A Fair Guide to Credit Repair
by Mark Lyvers

Table of Contents

How FICO scores are calculated?

The 609 Loophole

Chapter 1: Dealing with Debt

Chapter 2: Statute of Limitations

Chapter 3: Credit Bureaus

Chapter 4: Forms

Chapter 5: Good Credit

Chapter 6: Follow Up

Chapter 7: Putting it to Use

Preface

I wrote this book because I know firsthand how hard it can be to fix damaged credit. I also know that there are not many people that will write a book about something they have experienced firsthand.

I wrote the book to help people. I wanted to keep the price affordable and the content straightforward and easy to understand.

People often do not try to fix things they do not understand.

They give up before they start.

I wrote this book for you.

Bibliography and reference

All the information gathered for this book is based on
common knowledge and the references for the book were
gathered from the **Fair Credit Reporting Act 1970 (F.C.R.A)**
And the amended act of 2010. And I have enclosed a copy of
the act in its entirety at the end of the book. Listed in the
Table of contents as chapter 6 Follow up.

A Fair Guide to Credit Repair by Mark Lyvers
The legal benefits of this guide are limited to the Fair Credit
Reporting Act 1970 (F.C.R.A)

The Fair Credit Act is a federal law for credit reporting
agencies. It compels them to ensure the information they
gather and distribute is "Fair" and "Accurate" when reporting
consumer credit histories.

I remember back in the 80's when I would just spend all my
money on B.S., and I didn't really understand what credit
was and I just figured it was for rich people and it didn't
affect me.

Credit is for everyone if used correctly, when I started to fix
my credit it was down in the 400's when I wanted to get a
home, I learned the magic numbers and I just needed to
figure out how to push my score up.

There are literally 100's of guides and books out there to
teach credit repair but you can be assured most of those
books were not written for you.

They were written by authors that just want to make money
and they don't really care about your situation or how to help
you out of it. My guide is more of a credit repair kit, it is full
of helpful information, I tell you how to write letters. Where
to send them and most importantly I have sample letters that
hundreds of people have used successfully to fix or repair
their own credit.
So, I mentioned earlier the magic numbers. 850 is the highest
credit score you can get. Mine is around 810 to 815 it
fluctuates a little every month sometimes it goes down a
couple points or it goes up a couple points.

If you want to buy a home, you need a minimum score of 620 for most banks. 620 doesn't mean you're getting the best rate it just means that, that is the starting point. I recommend you shoot for 725 as your magic number because when you see the best rate available that is the rate you want. Anything over 750 puts you I the top 1% of credit holders in America, it basically means you can buy anything you want if you can prove you can afford to make the payment.

The main point I want to drive home is this, I know what it feels like to have no credit, and I know what it takes to have amazing credit. I am going to teach you how to fix your credit, how to build positive credit, how to add positive credit to your report. Creditors will generally never teach you this because the elite 1% don't really want everyone being able to rise and get the best rates on anything. Cars, Boats, Homes, Rv's , whatever it is you want, if your score is high enough you can enjoy the finer things in life even if you're not rich.

You have rights, and you can do it yourself in many cases you may not need to hire an outside agency to help you. Generally, you can expect somewhat quicker changes doing it yourself because there are no wait times. You will likely send in the forms and not stall them, but I will say this if you send in the forms I premade during tax time, there is a good chance that they will be accepted. Why? Because when you send in your forms, they are sent in with thousands of other people that know when to mail them. It's kind of like a lottery sort of, the credit reporting agencies only have so much time to investigate each case and if they miss the deadline, they have to clear the debt from the report but we will get into that later.

I am writing this book to protect you not the creditor, they didn't buy my book you did. So, while you read this you will see, I will side with you. I am going to help you not the creditor.

You will need the information contained in this guide to get it done. I have prepared forms, and information to help you on your journey to fixing or repairing your negative credit as well as helping you to maintain good credit habits in the future.

Legal Disclaimer,
Each person's credit situation is unique. Results may vary, and this credit repair guide makes no guarantee of any particular result. The information in this guide intended for general informational purposes only, and is not to be construed as legal, tax, accounting, or other professional advice. As such, it should not be used as, or relied upon, as a substitute for seeking professional legal, tax, accounting, or other advice. All information in this guide is provided "as-is", with no guarantee of completeness, accuracy, timeliness, or other results obtained from its use.

In no event shall the guidebook author, or company be liable to you or anyone else for any decision made or action taken in reliance on the information in this guidebook. You agree that you take full responsibility for your own actions and agree to hold harmless the writers of this guide.

Credit Repair is always changing, now we are still using the older system with the big 3 reporting agencies but the way they calculate the score has changed.

FICO Scores are calculated using many different pieces of credit data in your credit report. This data is grouped into five categories: payment history (35%), amounts owed (30%), length of credit history (15%), new credit (10%) and credit mix (10%).

The older system was based on your payment history Vs the total credit lines you had and now it's been revamped. So, it's even more important to understand how it all works for all of us.

So literally if you were 3 or 4 points away from getting your new home you may be able to open a new credit card and push up your score because 10% of your score is based on new credit.

Sometimes it's just knowing the little things that can change your life. I hope you take the time to enjoy this book.

So, let's take a closer look at the categories for a FICO score

35% Payments this is the first thing a creditor looks at, are you paying your bills, most creditors will only look 3 pages into a credit report assuming that the whole report is the same.

Why is this important? Because it may be possible to pad the first three pages of a credit report in your favor. More on that later. See adding positive credit later in the book for more ideas on how to do that.

Credit repair used to take 12 to 24 months but really it can take 3 to 6 months in some cases. So, remember that if you decide to hire a company to do it for you when they drag you along month after month siphoning your money.

Amounts owed (30%) this is based on your over all credit if you have 100k in credit and use 30% of it , you have a ton of debt to credit ratio and it will drop your score significantly, but if you use only 2% of 100k you still have plenty of money available that is not being used and that will push your score up. So I think the idea here is simple just because you have a credit card doesn't mean you need to use it.

Length of credit history (15%) this used to be way more of a influencer on your credit score but now its not and having new credit (10%) and credit that is not old is now blended into a mixed category and only accounts for (10%) of the credit score.

Why is this good?
It's great for younger people that are just starting out, it means that more creditors will help them when they have little or no credit and it will allow the credit to grow more rapidly. Meaning younger adults may qualify for homes and car purchases early on and not have to wait to buy goods and services.

Understanding the 609 Loophole

In section 609 and 611 of the F.D.R.A there is a requirement that creditors must follow on investigations. This is perhaps the very best information anyone will ever give you for $14.

Remember when I told you I am here for you well I am, and I have seen people charging hundreds of dollars for this information online.

You do not need a special template to use this for a letter, I have already included the pre-written example. So, let's get into it, it's a little tricky but once you understand it, you will never forget it.

The 611 Dispute Letter often referred to as the 609 but if you dig into the law you will see the 609 clause has nothing to do with it but it is commonly known as the 609 Loophole.

The loophole occurs when you ask for information in your dispute letter that is unverifiable and because the credit bureau is unable to verify the information, they must remove the item from your credit report.

The theory is if you ask the credit bureaus for information, they clearly cannot produce like the original signed copies of your credit applications. The cashed checks used for bill payments. Etcetera, then they would have to remove the disputed item because it's unverifiable.

You could just say in your letter at the top of the page "According to the F.D.R.A I have the right to dispute any claims against my credit report."

Your going to hear people say this is full proof well it isn't but it does work more often than not and therefor it is worth exploring.

So, let's take a closer look into what you might say in a dispute letter. You will find that letter template on page 33

Don't just skip everything else, you do need to keep reading.

Chapter 1: Dealing with Debt

Getting started, if you have negative credit it may be safe to assume that you have been contacted by a creditor or a debt collector to collect the debt.

Do not be in a hurry to immediately pay the debt.

Yes, you heard me, slow down and check this out.

Remember I am here for you and there is a process that can potentially save you thousands of dollars.

You may not be aware that you have rights that protect you from being mistreated by creditors or debt collectors. Often these rights can vary from state to state. You will need to verify the accuracy of the information below.

The information is to be considered generally correct for all 50 states.

Debt collectors deal with debt everyday it's just another day at the office for them, but you may be stressed out, going crazy or just don't know what to do. Relax we got this!

Let's look at your rights, this may not cover all your rights, but it will cover the most often needed rights that you will need to protect yourself when dealing with debt.

1. You have a right to "Proof of Debt" if a collector reaches out to you, they must be able to prove the debt is yours. This means keep a pad of paper and a pen handy by the phone! Write down the date of the call, the time, who the person is and what company they are calling from. It is very likely that the person on the phone will have no idea that the timer has started because many people just like you do not know the law.

   You need to ask the creditor for "Proof of Debt". The creditor now has only 5 days to put the proof in writing and mail it to you.

   <u>You will not tell the creditor they have only 5 days</u> if they don't know the law that's their mistake not yours.

   If proof of debt is not established by the creditor within 5 days in writing. It may be possible to have the debt completely removed from your credit report whether you owe it or not.

<u>Do not admit to the debt over the phone</u> because they will record every conversation to collect the monies owed and the creditor will assume that the debt is yours.

You will tell the creditor **"I am not accepting the debt unless you can prove the debt is mine"**. Say nothing else, just wait for the reply.

It does not matter what the reply is, stay calm. In most cases the creditor will be in shock that you know the law and they will stumble along trying to get you to admit the debt is yours on the phone?

Tell them "I will wait for the proof by mail" thank them for the call and wish them a lovely day and hang up.

In some cases, the person on the phone will blow this off and not know that they only have 5 days to comply.

If the creditor does not provide "Proof of Debt" in writing within the 5day window.

You can petition the credit reporting agencies to remove the debt.

If the creditor sends you the proof within the 5-day window you have 30 days to dispute the debt. I recommend you dispute it even if you owe it.

Keep in mind I am not giving you legal advice but since you bought my book, I am going to tell you what I would do.

If you do dispute the debt the creditor or debt collector will investigate the debt and the debt collector must mail a copy of this verification or judgment to the consumer within a reasonable time frame.

According to the F.C.R.A a reasonable time frame is 30 days.

If the debt collector fails to send you verification or judgment to the consumer, within a 30-day window you may be able to have the debt removed from your credit report weather you, legitimately owe the debt or not.

If you choose not to dispute the debt after 30 days, the debt will be considered valid and the debt now belongs to you.

You have the right not to be harassed. You have a right to ask the collector if the call is being recorded and if it is you can inform them, they are also going to be recorded.

If you do advise them to make sure you get an ap on your phone that will record the call.

In many states it is perfectly legal to record a call if you make the other party aware of it.

If the creditor or the collector break any of the following guidelines and you can prove they did, you can sue or threaten to sue them under the F.C.R.A and it is likely that you will win, or they will just go away and you will never hear from them again.

It's important to understand you are not bound by these rules they are.

A creditor or debt collector may not call you on the phone before the hours of 8:00 AM and After 9:00 PM at night.

A creditor or debt collector may not swear on the phone or use crude or demeaning language.

A creditor or debt collector may not threaten you with deportation, bodily harm, arrest, firing, public shamming or anything else that is considered harmful or unprofessional.

Collectors may not discuss your debt with anyone else including leaving information about the debt on a answering machine.

Collectors may not pretend to be the police or the IRS

If a collector calls your work you can tell them, you cannot receive calls at work and by law they must stop. If they do not stop call an attorney.

The collector might settle out of court and agree to pay off your debt, it's worth a shot.

The collector might tell you; you need to put it in writing, and you can inform them you are recording the call and can prove you asked not to be called. Some states do require you to put it in writing and send it to the creditor via certified mail.

Chapter 2: **Statute of Limitations**

You have a right to have anything removed from your credit report that is 7 years or older except bankruptcies they will remain on your report for 10 years.

Statute of Limitations vary from state to state and can be as little as 3 to 7 years, so it is important to look it up and see if you have items that need to be removed.

Debt collectors get paid by collecting debt and will use tricks to get you to renew your debt.

WHAT!!! Yes, Pay Attention to this, it's very important.

They may say you need to make a goodwill payment on an old debt. As soon as you do that it renews the date of the old debt and now, they have another 7 years in some cases to collect on it.

Make sure before you pay any debt on your credit report that you look at the age of the debt and decide if you want to pay on it.

Any debt that is 12 to 24 months from charging off you may not want to pay on unless you can pay the balance in full. It is recommended that you seek legal advice before paying the bill.

If debt is older than 5 years old it may do more harm to your credit report to pay it, than it will to let it charge off.

Partial payments can also restart the legal liability of a debt, and or make it possible to sue or garnish wages on past debt if the debt is older than the statute of limitations.

You may feel you're doing a good thing, and have it come back to bite you later.

Court Summons on old debt. Never ignore this and assume that the statutes of limitations (SOL) will save you from having to pay it.

If you don't show up to court and show that the debt is old and outdated even if the SOL is up the court will find in favor of the collector and you will be forced to pay the debt often restarting the clock on the debts owed.

All you need is a copy of your credit report and a copy of the SOL for the state you are in. However, it is recommended that you have legal counsel if you ever step into a courtroom.

The collector will most definitely have counsel present and it may put you at a disadvantage if you do not.

It is important to understand that the SOL period starts when you fall behind on a debt or from the date of your last payment.

The length of the SOL AKA Statute of Limitations depends on state law for that type of debt. **Some types of debt have different SOL's.** Check with your state attorney general's office, a consumer law attorney, or legal aid, especially if you're threatened with legal action.

If you tell the debt collector not to contact you again, they are legally mandated to comply. It's always a good idea to put your request in writing or have a recording of the call.

Once the collector receives your written request, it can only contact you only to confirm that it received your request or notify you of legal action.

Note: Consumers who have been the subject of FDCPA violations can sue the collections agency in federal court and collect damages. Often, these suits will settle before trial.

If you are being aggressively pursued by a collection's agency, you should keep careful, detailed records of all communications.

Including but not limited to phone conversations, written documentation of violations and make sure you read the F.D.C.A to know all your rights and protections under the law.

False or misleading representations

A debt collector may not use any false, deceptive, or misleading representation or means in connection with the collection of any debt. Without limiting the general application of the foregoing, the following conduct is a violation of this section:

(1) The false representation or implication that the debt collector is vouched for, bonded by, or affiliated with the United States or any State, including the use of any badge, uniform, or facsimile thereof.

(2) The false representation of— (A)the character, amount, or legal status of any debt; or (B) any services rendered or compensation which may be lawfully received by any debt collector for the collection of a debt.

(3) The false representation or implication that any individual is an attorney or that any communication is from an attorney.

(4) The representation or implication that nonpayment of any debt will result in the arrest or imprisonment of any person or the seizure, garnishment, attachment, or sale of any property or wages of any person unless such action is lawful and the debt collector or creditor intends to take such action.

Settlements:

Settlements of debt are a slippery slope. You would think that settling the debt would be a benefit, but it can be harmful to your report still showing up as a negative mark on your credit report.

To make matters worse a settlement will renew the debt shown on your report for 7 more years even though it is paid. Showing a negative mark on your credit report.

So even though you paid your money to make it better it doesn't always make it better. It's kind of the stab in the back while you're walking out the door.

If you are going to settle a debt make sure you get the terms in writing and make sure that the creditor agrees in writing to remove the debt from your credit report when the payment is made. If it isn't in writing it isn't legal.

Do not take the creditors word over the phone that they will have the negative credit removed from your report, get it in writing.

Chapter 3: Credit Bureaus

Now it is time to get started in turning things around. Now that you know your basic rights under the F.D.C.A it's time to start putting the pieces together.

In the U.S., there are three national credit bureaus (Equifax, Experian and TransUnion) that compete to capture, update and store credit histories on most U.S. consumers.

You will need a copy of your credit report to get started. Now Equifax, Experian and TransUnion may not all share the same information.

If you pull your credit history from each of these companies and if you happen to notice that one or two are missing a delinquent account, it is not recommended that you make them aware of this. It will only hurt your credit score, however if you have good credit that is not being reported to each creditor it is recommended that you do report it to each creditor.

How do I get a copy of my credit report?

Credit Bureau	Mailing Address	Phone Number
TransUnion	P.O. Box 1000 Chester, PA 19022	1-800-916-8800
Equifax	P.O. Box 740241 Atlanta, GA 30374-0241	1-800-685-1111
Experian	P.O. Box 2104 Allen, TX 75013-0949	1-888-397-3742

Big 3 Credit Bureaus

Call each of them on the phone and find out how to get a copy of your credit report.

Once you have a copy continue with this guide to start turning things around!

Once you receive a copy of your credit reports pay close attention to them because sometimes people with the same name as yours may have their delinquent accounts on your credit history.

If you feel the reports are inaccurate for any reason you can file a dispute and we will get to that later.

I want you to understand that there are things that you can do to help your situation and I will try to cover them in this guide.

Not only can you dispute a credit error but you can also add good credit, you can add notes to your accounts, you have as much control on your credit reports as the creditors do, they just don't want you to know about it.

As explained earlier you have rights! It is time to take control of your situation and stop allowing bad credit to stop you from enjoying the finer things that life has to offer.

There are 2 different ways to dispute an error on the website or in the mail if you decided you want to dispute via paper you can but you must send the letter via certified mail or it will not be accepted.

To send a dispute via the mail you can use the above addresses and the following letter.

Chapter 4: The Forms

These are all the forms you need feel free to remove them
from the book and make copies and use them.

As far as I know you do not need to have a full sheet of paper
to fill in a form and mail it into a credit bureau but for each
for you decide to use you will need 3 because you will want
to mail one to each credit bureau

Attach copy of your credit report to the letter and circle the
account or accounts you wish to be removed, repaired or
added. If you send in a letter that is not certified mail it will
be tossed out and never read.

Make sure you mail it the correct way and always ask for a
receipt, so you have proof of a timeline from when they
received it.

You will get the receipt from the post office not the credit
bureau so they can't say they didn't get your request.

Do not use the forms in this book, make copies of them and
use them for every dispute you will need 4 copies. One for
each credit bureau and one for your records.

Date:

Re: Request for Correction

Dear Credit Reporting Agency

I have received a copy of my credit report supplied by your company.

I am attaching a copy of the credit report with an inaccuracy circled.

Please reinvestigate the noted information and make the changes I have indicated.

After the changes are made please send me a free copy of my credit report noting the changes.

Also please limit your investigation to a "reasonable time" (30 days) as required by law.

Respectfully,
Your Name:
Address:
Phone number:
SS#:

Date:

Re: Request to Delete Account

Dear Credit Reporting Agency

I was contacted by a third party collector named
________________ they contacted me on
Day__________________ Date ________________ At Time
______________ but failed to provide proof of debt within the 5
day window as required by the F.C.R.A
because of this I would like to request the circled account on
my credit report to be deleted from my account.

I do not believe the account is mine and because the creditor /
third party collector was unable to provide me with "Proof of
Debt" as required by the Law.

I would like it to be expunged from my record ASAP and I
would like a free copy of my new credit report showing the
changes made.

Thank you in advance in getting this taken care of in a
reasonable time frame (30 days) as required by law.

Respectfully,
Your name
Address
Phone #
SS#

Date:

Re: Request to add a consumer statement

In accordance with the F.C.R.A I have a right to add a consumer statement into my credit report.

I have disputed and noted accounts and since the reinvestigation has not resolved my dispute, I want the following statement entered on my account setting forth the nature of my dispute for others to see.

____
____
____
____
____

I assume that 30 days constitutes a reasonable time to include this into my report unless you notify me immediately. In accordance to the F.C.R..A please send me an updated free copy of my credit report with the changes noted.

Respectfully,
Your name,
Address
Phone #
SS#

Date:

Dear Credit Reporting Agency,

I wish to exercise my right under section 609 of the F.D.R.A
to request information regarding an item that is listed on my
consumer credit report.

I have included the credit report and circled the item I wish to
dispute.

As per Section 609 of the Fair Debt Reporting Act, I am
entitled to see the source of the information, which is the
original contract with my signature.

My identifying information is as follows
Date of Birth _______________________
SSN _____________________________________

As Proof of my identity I have included a copy of my Social
security Card and my Birth Certificate.

If you are unable to verify the account with the original
contract, the information should be removed from my credit
report within 30 days.

Respectfully, ____
Signature, ____
Address____

____
Phone # ____
SS#____

If you decide to use the 609 Loophole Letter make sure you make 3 copies and include a copy of your SS Card and your Birth Certificate send it via Certified mail and request a receipt so you can prove the 30 day window is not met.

Send one copy to each credit bureau and keep a copy for your records.

If you are one of those people that say I don't need to give anyone my social security number.

Do not even bother sending this in, believe me when I say they already have it. If you do not include it, it will be rejected and tossed in the trash.

Chapter 5: Good Credit!

Anyone can be a creditor even your dad.

If anyone has ever loaned you money and you paid them back guess what that is a credit line or a line of credit. Just because you're not dealing with a bank doesn't mean that regular people are not lenders because they are. All you need is a account number and the other person to verify the loan when the creditors call to verify the loan and payment information.

All you need to do is write a letter to the credit bureaus. It should look like this.

This is one your going to write yourself and not use this template, but I have included one that you can use as a reference.

Dear Credit Reporting Agency

On _________ a loan was made to me by ___________ in the

amount of $___________all the payments were made in a

timely manner and the final payment was made on _________.

Here are the specifics. I would like this information verified
and added to my credit file.

____

____

____

____

____

____

____

____

____

Account Number _______________________________

Duration of the loan ____________________________ months

Lenders name, address, and phone
number____

____

Borrowers Information
Name
Address
Phone
SS#
D.O.B
Signature

____

The credit bureaus have an obligation under the law to verify
this is true and they must add it to your credit report it is the
law. You can use the same lender multiple times, you can use
your electric company, you can use a car rental, you can use
anyone that has ever extended credit to you.

Think about this you could use your dad 5 times if you
wanted to it doesn't matter under the law they have to verify
the information and report it because it is their job, you will
want to submit this information to all 3 credit bureaus and
then you will notice your credit begin to go up.

Literally what you need to do is to push the old credit behind
the new good credit and over time you will see your credit
score rise. I recommend you do this a min of 5 times not to
exceed 10 entries per year. could do it 20 times if you wanted
to but at some point it will begin to look suspicious so add
any utilities any time someone loaned you money anything at
all and keep submitting them till you reach the amount you
feel is good enough.

Be honest and fair because credit scores effect all of us.

Chapter 6: Follow Up

Here is the whole copy of the
"Fair Debt Reporting Act of 1970 with the 2010
Amendment"

I am enclosing this for your information as a reference in
case you wish to read it for a better understanding of your
rights and protections.

THE FAIR DEBT COLLECTION PRACTICES ACT as amended by Pub. L. 111-203, title X, 124 Stat. 2092 (2010) As a public service, the staff of the Federal Trade Commission (FTC) has prepared the following complete text of the Fair Debt Collection Practices Act (FDCPA), 15 U.S.C. §§ 1692-1692p. Please note that the format of the text differs in minor ways from the U.S. Code and West's U.S. Code Annotated. For example, this version uses FDCPA section numbers in the headings. In addition, the relevant U.S. Code citation is included with each section heading. Although the staff has made every effort to transcribe the statutory material accurately, this compendium is intended as a convenience for the public and not a substitute for the text in the U.S. Code. Table of Contents § 801 Short title § 802 Congressional findings and declaration of purpose § 803 Definitions § 804 Acquisition of location information § 805 Communication in connection with debt collection § 806 Harassment or abuse § 807 False or misleading representations § 808 Unfair practices § 809 Validation of debts § 810 Multiple debts § 811 Legal actions by debt collectors § 812 Furnishing certain deceptive forms § 813 Civil liability § 814 Administrative enforcement § 815 Reports to Congress by the Bureau; views of other Federal agencies § 816 Relation to State laws § 817 Exemption for State regulation § 818 Exception for certain bad check enforcement programs operated by private entities § 819 Effective date 2 § 801 15 USC 1601 note § 801. Short Title This subchapter may be cited as the "Fair Debt Collection Practices Act." § 802. Congressional findings and declaration of purpose (a) Abusive practices There is abundant evidence of the use of abusive, deceptive, and unfair debt collection practices by many debt collectors. Abusive debt collection practices contribute to the number of personal bankruptcies, to marital instability, to the loss of jobs, and to invasions of individual privacy. (b) Inadequacy of laws Existing laws and procedures for redressing these injuries are inadequate to protect consumers. (c) Available non-abusive collection methods Means other than misrepresentation or other abusive debt collection practices are available for the effective collection of debts. (d) Interstate commerce Abusive debt collection practices are carried on to a substantial extent in interstate commerce and through means and instrumentalities of such commerce. Even where abusive debt collection practices are purely intrastate in character, they nevertheless directly affect interstate commerce. (e) Purposes It is the purpose of this subchapter to eliminate abusive debt collection practices by debt collectors, to insure that those debt collectors who refrain from using abusive debt collection practices are not competitively disadvantaged, and to promote consistent State action to protect consumers against debt collection abuses. 15 USC 1601 note 15 USC 1692 3 § 803 15 USC 1692a § 803. Definitions As used in this subchapter—

(1) The term "Bureau" means the Bureau of Consumer Financial Protection.

(2) The term "communication" means the conveying of information regarding a debt directly or indirectly to any person through any medium.

(3) The term "consumer" means any natural person obligated or allegedly obligated to pay any debt.

(4) The term "creditor" means any person who offers or extends credit creating a debt or to whom a debt is owed, but such term does not include any person to the extent that he receives an assignment or transfer of a debt in default solely for the purpose of facilitating collection of such debt for another.

(5) The term "debt" means any obligation or alleged obligation of a consumer to pay money arising out of a transaction in which the money, property, insurance or services which are the subject of the transaction are primarily for personal, family, or household purposes, whether or not such obligation has been reduced to judgment. (6) The term "debt collector" means any person who uses any instrumentality of interstate commerce or the mails in any business the principal purpose of which is the collection of any debts, or who regularly collects or attempts to collect, directly or indirectly, debts owed or due or asserted to be owed or due another. Notwithstanding the exclusion provided by clause (F) of the last sentence of this paragraph, the term includes any creditor who, in the process of collecting his own debts, uses any name other than his own which would indicate that a third person is collecting or attempting to collect such debts. For the purpose of section 1692f(6) of this title, such term also includes any person who uses any instrumentality of interstate commerce or the mails in any business the principal pur15 USC 1692a 4 § 803 15 USC 1692a pose of which is the enforcement of security interests. The term does not include— (A) any officer or employee of a creditor while, in the name of the creditor, collecting debts for such creditor; (B) any person while acting as a debt collector for another person, both of whom are related by common ownership or affiliated by corporate control, if the person acting as a debt collector does so only for persons to whom it is so related or affiliated and if the principal business of such person is not the collection of debts; (C) any officer or employee of the United States or any State to the extent that collecting or attempting to collect any debt is in the performance of his official duties; (D) any person while serving or attempting to serve legal process on any other person in connection with the judicial enforcement of any debt; (E) any nonprofit organization which, at the request of consumers, performs bona fide consumer credit counseling

and assists consumers in the liquidation of their debts by receiving payments from such consumers and distributing such amounts to creditors; and (F) any person collecting or attempting to collect any debt owed or due or asserted to be owed or due another to the extent such activity (i) is incidental to a bona fide fiduciary obligation or a bona fide escrow arrangement; (ii) concerns a debt which was originated by such person; (iii) concerns a debt which was not in default at the time it was obtained by such person; or (iv) concerns a debt obtained by such person as a secured party in a commercial credit transaction involving the creditor. 5 § 803 15 USC 1692a (7) The term "location information" means a consumer's place of abode and his telephone number at such place, or his place of employment. (8) The term "State" means any State, territory, or possession of the United States, the District of Columbia, the Commonwealth of Puerto Rico, or any political subdivision of any of the foregoing. § 804. Acquisition of location information Any debt collector communicating with any person other than the consumer for the purpose of acquiring location information about the consumer shall—

(1) identify himself, state that he is confirming or correcting location information concerning the consumer, and, only if expressly requested, identify his employer; (2) not state that such consumer owes any debt; (3) not communicate with any such person more than once unless requested to do so by such person or unless the debt collector reasonably believes that the earlier response of such person is erroneous or incomplete and that such person now has correct or complete location information; (4) not communicate by post card; (5) not use any language or symbol on any envelope or in the contents of any communication effected by the mails or telegram that indicates that the debt collector is in the debt collection business or that the communication relates to the collection of a debt; and (6) after the debt collector knows the consumer is represented by an attorney with regard to the subject debt and has knowledge of, or can readily ascertain, such attorney's name and address, not communicate with any person other than that attorney, unless the attorney fails to respond within a reasonable period of time to communication from the debt collector. 15 USC 1692b 6 § 805 15 USC 1692c § 805. Communication in connection with debt collection (a) Communication with the consumer generally Without the prior consent of the consumer given directly to the debt collector or the express permission of a court of competent jurisdiction, a debt collector may not communicate with a consumer in connection with the collection of any debt—

(1) at any unusual time or place or a time or place known, or which should be known to be inconvenient to the consumer. In the absence of knowledge of circumstances to the contrary, a debt collector shall assume that the convenient time for communicating with a consumer is after 8 o'clock antemeridian and before 9 o'clock postmeridian, local time at the consumer's location; (2) if the debt collector knows the consumer is represented by an attorney with respect to such debt and has knowledge of, or can readily ascertain, such attorney's name and address, unless the attorney fails to respond within a reasonable period of time to a communication from the debt collector or unless the attorney consents to direct communication with the consumer; or (3) at the consumer's place of employment if the debt collector knows or has reason to know that the consumer's employer prohibits the consumer from receiving such communication. (b) Communication with third parties Except as provided in section 1692b of this title, without the prior consent of the consumer given directly to the debt collector, or the express permission of a court of competent jurisdiction, or as reasonably necessary to effectuate a post judgment judicial remedy, a debt collector may not communicate, in connection with the collection of any debt, with any person other than the consumer, his attorney, a consumer reporting agency if otherwise permitted by law, the creditor, the attorney of the creditor, or the attorney of the debt collector. (c) Ceasing communication 15 USC 1692c 7 § 805 15 USC 1692c If a consumer notifies a debt collector in writing that the consumer refuses to pay a debt or that the consumer wishes the debt collector to cease further communication with the consumer, the debt collector shall not communicate further with the consumer with respect to such debt, except—

(1) to advise the consumer that the debt collector's further efforts are being terminated; (2) to notify the consumer that the debt collector or creditor may invoke specified remedies which are ordinarily invoked by such debt collector or creditor; or (3) where applicable, to notify the consumer that the debt collector or creditor intends to invoke a specified remedy. If such notice from the consumer is made by mail, notification shall be complete upon receipt. (d) "Consumer" defined For the purpose of this section, the term "consumer" includes the consumer's spouse, parent (if the consumer is a minor), guardian, executor, or administrator. § 806. Harassment or abuse A debt collector may not engage in any conduct the natural consequence of which is to harass, oppress, or abuse any person in connection with the collection of a debt. Without limiting the general application of the foregoing, the following conduct is a violation of this section:

(1) The use or threat of use of violence or other criminal means to harm the physical person, reputation, or property of any person. (2) The use of obscene or profane language or language the natural consequence of which is to abuse the hearer or reader. (3) The publication of a list of consumers who allegedly refuse to pay debts, except to a consumer reporting agency or to persons meeting the requirements of sec15 USC 1692d 8 § 806 15 USC 1692d tion 1681a(f) or 1681b(3)1 of this title. (4) The advertisement for sale of any debt to coerce payment of the debt. (5) Causing a telephone to ring or engaging any person in telephone conversation repeatedly or continuously with intent to annoy, abuse, or harass any person at the called number. (6)Except as provided in section 1692b of this title, the placement of telephone calls without meaningful disclosure of the caller's identity. § 807. False or misleading representations A debt collector may not use any false, deceptive, or misleading representation or means in connection with the collection of any debt. Without limiting the general application of the foregoing, the following conduct is a violation of this section:

(1) The false representation or implication that the debt collector is vouched for, bonded by, or affiliated with the United States or any State, including the use of any badge, uniform, or facsimile thereof. (2) The false representation of— (A)the character, amount, or legal status of any debt; or (B) any services rendered or compensation which may be lawfully received by any debt collector for the collection of a debt. (3) The false representation or implication that any individual is an attorney or that any communication is from an attorney. (4) The representation or implication that nonpayment of any debt will result in the arrest or imprisonment of any person or the seizure, garnishment, attachment, or sale of any property or wages of any person unless such action is lawful and the debt collector or creditor intends to take such action. 1. Section 604(3) has been renumbered as Section 604(a)(3). 15 USC 1692e 9 § 807 15 USC 1692e (5) The threat to take any action that cannot legally be taken or that is not intended to be taken. (6) The false representation or implication that a sale, referral, or other transfer of any interest in a debt shall cause the consumer to— (A) lose any claim or defense to payment of the debt; or (B) become subject to any practice prohibited by this subchapter. (7) The false representation or implication that the consumer committed any crime or other conduct in order to disgrace the consumer. (8) Communicating or threatening to communicate to any person credit information which is known or which should be known to be false, including the failure to communicate that a disputed debt is disputed. (9) The use or distribution of any written communication which simulates or is falsely represented to be a document authorized, issued, or approved by any court, official, or agency of the United States or any State, or which creates a false impression as to its source, authorization, or approval. (10) The use of any false representation or deceptive means to collect or attempt to collect any debt or to obtain information concerning a consumer. (11) The failure

to disclose in the initial written communication with the consumer and, in addition, if the initial communication with the consumer is oral, in that initial oral communication, that the debt collector is attempting to collect a debt and that any information obtained will be used for that purpose, and the failure to disclose in subsequent communications that the communication is from a debt collector, except that this paragraph shall not apply to a formal pleading made in connection with a legal action. (12) The false representation or implication that accounts have been turned over to innocent purchasers for value. 10 § 807 15 USC 1692e (13) The false representation or implication that documents are legal process. (14) The use of any business, company, or organization name other than the true name of the debt collector's business, company, or organization. (15) The false representation or implication that documents are not legal process forms or do not require action by the consumer. (16) The false representation or implication that a debt collector operates or is employed by a consumer reporting agency as defined by section 1681a(f) of this title. § 808. Unfair practices A debt collector may not use unfair or unconscionable means to collect or attempt to collect any debt. Without limiting the general application of the foregoing, the following conduct is a violation of this section:

(1) The collection of any amount (including any interest, fee, charge, or expense incidental to the principal obligation) unless such amount is expressly authorized by the agreement creating the debt or permitted by law. (2) The acceptance by a debt collector from any person of a check or other payment instrument postdated by more than five days unless such person is notified in writing of the debt collector's intent to deposit such check or instrument not more than ten nor less than three business days prior to such deposit. (3) The solicitation by a debt collector of any postdated check or other postdated payment instrument for the purpose of threatening or instituting criminal prosecution. (4) Depositing or threatening to deposit any postdated check or other postdated payment instrument prior to the date on such check or instrument. (5) Causing charges to be made to any person for communications by concealment of the true propose of the communication. Such charges include, but are not limited to, collect telephone calls and telegram fees. 15 USC 1692f 11 § 808 15 USC 1692f (6) Taking or threatening to take any nonjudicial action to effect dispossession or disablement of property if— (A)there is no present right to possession of the property claimed as collateral through an enforceable security interest; (B) there is no present intention to take possession of the property; or (C) the property is exempt by law from such dispossession or disablement. (7) Communicating with a consumer regarding a debt by post card. (8) Using any language or symbol, other than the debt collector's address, on any envelope when communicating with a consumer by use of the mails or by telegram, except that a debt collector may use his business name if such name does not indicate that he is in the debt collection business. § 809. Validation of debts (a) Notice of debt; contents Within five days after the initial communication with a consumer in connection with the collection of any debt, a debt collector shall, unless the following information is contained in the initial communication or the consumer has paid the debt,

send the consumer a written notice containing—
(1) the amount of the debt; (2) the name of the creditor to whom the debt is owed; (3) a statement that unless the consumer, within thirty days after receipt of the notice, disputes the validity of the debt, or any portion thereof, the debt will be assumed to be valid by the debt collector; (4) a statement that if the consumer notifies the debt collector in writing within the thirty-day period that the debt, or any portion thereof, is disputed, the debt collector will obtain verification of the debt or a copy of a judgment against the consumer and a copy of such 15 USC 1692g 12 § 809 15 USC 1692g verification or judgment will be mailed to the consumer by the debt collector; and (5) a statement that, upon the consumer's written request within the thirty-day period, the debt collector will provide the consumer with the name and address of the original creditor, if different from the current creditor. (b) Disputed debts If the consumer notifies the debt collector in writing within the thirty-day period described in subsection (a) of this section that the debt, or any portion thereof, is disputed, or that the consumer requests the name and address of the original creditor, the debt collector shall cease collection of the debt, or any disputed portion thereof, until the debt collector obtains verification of the debt or a copy of a judgment, or the name and address of the original creditor, and a copy of such verification or judgment, or name and address of the original creditor, is mailed to the consumer by the debt collector.

Collection activities and communications that do not otherwise violate this subchapter may continue during the 30-day period referred to in subsection (a) unless the consumer has notified the debt collector in writing that the debt, or any portion of the debt, is disputed or that the consumer requests the name and address of the original creditor.

Any collection activities and communication during the 30-day period may not overshadow or be inconsistent with the disclosure of the consumer's right to dispute the debt or request the name and address of the original creditor. (c) Admission of liability The failure of a consumer to dispute the validity of a debt under this section may not be construed by any court as an admission of liability by the consumer. (d) Legal pleadings A communication in the form of a formal pleading in a civil action shall not be treated as an initial communication for purposes of subsection (a). 13 § 809 15 USC 1692g (e) Notice provisions The sending or delivery of any form or notice which does not relate to the collection of a debt and is expressly required by title 26, title V of Gramm-Leach-Bliley Act [15 U.S.C. 6801 et seq.], or any provision of Federal or State law relating to notice of data security breach or privacy, or any regulation prescribed under any such provision of law, shall not be treated as an initial communication in connection with debt collection for purposes of this section. § 810. Multiple debts If any consumer owes multiple debts and makes any single payment to any debt collector with respect to such debts, such debt collector may not apply such payment to any debt which is disputed by the consumer and, where applicable, shall apply such payment in accordance with the consumer's directions. § 811. Legal actions by debt collectors (a) Venue Any debt collector who brings any legal action on a debt against any consumer shall— (1) in the case of an action to enforce an interest in real property securing the consumer's obligation, bring such action only in a judicial district or similar legal entity in which such real property is located; or (2) in the case of an action not described in paragraph (1), bring such action only in the judicial district or similar legal entity— (A)in which such consumer signed the contract sued upon; or (B) in which such consumer resides at the commencement of the action. (b) Authorization of actions Nothing in this subchapter shall be construed to authorize the bringing of legal actions by debt collectors. 15 USC 1692i 15 USC 1692h 14 § 812 15 USC 1692j § 812. Furnishing certain deceptive forms (a) It is unlawful to design, compile, and furnish any form knowing that such form would be used to create the false belief in a consumer that a person other than the creditor of such consumer is participating in the collection of or in an attempt to collect a debt such consumer allegedly owes such creditor, when in fact such person is not so participating. (b) Any person who violates this section shall be liable to the same extent and in the same manner as a debt collector is liable under section 1692k of this title for failure to comply with a provision of this subchapter. § 813. Civil liability (a) Amount of damages Except as otherwise provided by this section, any debt collector who fails to comply with any provision of this subchapter with respect to any person is liable to such person in an amount equal to the sum of—

(1) any actual damage sustained by such person as a result of such failure; (2) (A) in the case of any action by an individual, such additional damages as the court may allow, but not exceeding $1,000; or (B) in the case of a class action, (i) such amount for each named plaintiff as could be recovered under subparagraph (A), and (ii) such amount as the court may allow for all other class members, without regard to a minimum individual recovery, not to exceed the lesser of $500,000 or 1 per centum of the net worth of the debt collector; and (3) in the case of any successful action to enforce the foregoing liability, the costs of the action, together with a reasonable attorney's fee as determined by the court. On a finding by the court that an action under this sec15 USC 1692k 15 USC 1692j 15 § 813 15 USC 1692ktion was brought in bad faith and for the purpose of harassment, the court may award to the defendant attorney's fees reasonable in relation to the work expended and costs. (b) Factors considered by court In determining the amount of liability in any action under subsection (a) of this section, the court shall consider, among other relevant factors—

(1) in any individual action under subsection (a)(2)(A) of this section, the frequency and persistence of noncompliance by the debt collector, the nature of such noncompliance, and the extent to which such noncompliance was intentional; or (2) in any class action under subsection (a)(2)(B) of this section, the frequency and persistence of noncompliance by the debt collector, the nature of such noncompliance, the resources of the debt collector, the number of persons adversely affected, and the extent to which the debt collector's noncompliance was intentional. (c) Intent A debt collector may not be held liable in any action brought under this subchapter if the debt collector shows by a preponderance of evidence that the violation was not intentional and resulted from a bona fide error notwithstanding the maintenance of procedures reasonably adapted to avoid any such error. (d) Jurisdiction An action to enforce any liability created by this subchapter may be brought in any appropriate United States district court without regard to the amount in controversy, or in any other court of competent jurisdiction, within one year from the date on which the violation occurs. (e) Advisory opinions of Bureau No provision of this section imposing any liability shall apply to any act done or omitted in good faith in conformity with any advisory opinion of the Bureau, not with- 16 § 813 15 USC 1692k standing that after such act or omission has occurred, such opinion is amended, rescinded, or determined by judicial or other authority to be invalid for any reason. § 814. Administrative enforcement (a) Federal Trade Commission The Federal Trade Commission shall be authorized to enforce compliance with this subchapter, except to the extent that enforcement of the requirements imposed under this subchapter is specifically committed to another Government agency under any of paragraphs (1) through (5) of subsection (b), subject to subtitle B of the Consumer Financial Protection Act of 2010 [12 U.S.C. 5511 et seq.]. For purpose of the exercise by the Federal Trade Commission of its functions and powers under the Federal

Trade Commission Act (15 U.S.C. 41 et seq.), a violation of this subchapter shall be deemed an unfair or deceptive act or practice in violation of that Act. All of the functions and powers of the Federal Trade Commission under the Federal Trade Commission Act are available to the Federal Trade Commission to enforce compliance by any person with this subchapter, irrespective of whether that person is engaged in commerce or meets any other jurisdictional tests under the Federal Trade Commission Act, including the power to enforce the provisions of this subchapter, in the same manner as if the violation had been a violation of a Federal Trade Commission trade regulation rule. (b) Applicable provisions of law Subject to subtitle B of the Consumer Financial Protection Act of 2010, compliance with any requirements imposed under this subchapter shall be enforced under—

(1) section 8 of the Federal Deposit Insurance Act [12 U.S.C. 1818], by the appropriate Federal banking agency, as defined in section 3(q) of the Federal Deposit Insurance Act (12 U.S.C. 1813(q)), with respect to— 15 USC 16921 17 (A)national banks, Federal savings associations, and Federal branches and Federal agencies of foreign banks; (B) member banks of the Federal Reserve System (other than national banks), branches and agencies of foreign banks (other than Federal branches, Federal agencies, and insured State branches of foreign banks), commercial lending companies owned or controlled by foreign banks, and organizations operating under section 25 or 25A of the Federal Reserve Act [12 U.S.C. 601 et seq., 611 et seq.]; and (C) banks and State savings associations insured by the Federal Deposit Insurance Corporation (other than members of the Federal Reserve System), and insured State branches of foreign banks; (2) the Federal Credit Union Act [12 U.S.C. 1751 et seq.], by the Administrator of the National Credit Union Administration with respect to any Federal credit union; (3) subtitle IV of title 49, by the Secretary of Transportation, with respect to all carriers subject to the jurisdiction of the Surface Transportation Board; (4) part A of subtitle VII of title 49, by the Secretary of Transportation with respect to any air carrier or any foreign air carrier subject to that part; (5) the Packers and Stockyards Act, 1921 [7 U.S.C. 181 et seq.] (except as provided in section 406 of that Act [7 U.S.C. 226, 227]), by the Secretary of Agriculture with respect to any activities subject to that Act; and (6) subtitle E of the Consumer Financial Protection Act of 2010 [12 U.S.C. 5561 et seq.], by the Bureau, with respect to any person subject to this subchapter. The terms used in paragraph (1) that are not defined in this subchapter or otherwise defined in section 3(s) of the Federal Deposit Insurance Act (12 U.S.C. 1813(s)) shall have the meaning given to them in section 1(b) of the International Banking Act of 1978 (12 U.S.C. 3101). § 814 15 USC 16921 18 (c) Agency powers For the purpose of the

exercise by any agency referred to in subsection (b) of this section of its powers under any Act referred to in that subsection, a violation of any requirement imposed under this subchapter shall be deemed to be a violation of a requirement imposed under that Act. In addition to its powers under any provision of law specifically referred to in subsection (b) of this section, each of the agencies referred to in that subsection may exercise, for the purpose of enforcing compliance with any requirement imposed under this subchapter any other authority conferred on it by law, except as provided in subsection (d) of this section. (d) Rules and regulations Except as provided in section 1029(a) of the Consumer Financial Protection Act of 2010 [12 U.S.C. 5519(a)], the Bureau may prescribe rules with respect to the collection of debts by debt collectors, as defined in this subchapter. § 815. Reports to Congress by the Bureau; views of other Federal agencies (a) Not later than one year after the effective date of this subchapter and at one-year intervals thereafter, the Bureau shall make reports to the Congress concerning the administration of its functions under this subchapter, including such recommendations as the Bureau deems necessary or appropriate. In addition, each report of the Bureau shall include its assessment of the extent to which compliance with this subchapter is being achieved and a summary of the enforcement actions taken by the Bureau under section 1692l of this title. (b) In the exercise of its functions under this subchapter, the Bureau may obtain upon request the views of any other Federal agency which exercises enforcement functions under section 1692l of this title. 15 USC 1692m § 814 15 USC 1692l 19 § 816 15 USC 1692n § 816. Relation to State laws This subchapter does not annul, alter, or affect, or exempt any person subject to the provisions of this subchapter from complying with the laws of any State with respect to debt collection practices, except to the extent that those laws are inconsistent with any provision of this subchapter, and then only to the extent of the inconsistency. For purposes of this section, a State law is not inconsistent with this subchapter if the protection such law affords any consumer is greater than the protection provided by this subchapter. § 817. Exemption for State regulation The Bureau shall by regulation exempt from the requirements of this subchapter any class of debt collection practices within any State if the Bureau determines that under the law of that State that class of debt collection practices is subject to requirements substantially similar to those imposed by this subchapter, and that there is adequate provision for enforcement. § 818. Exception for certain bad check enforcement programs operated by private entities (a) In general

(1) Treatment of certain private entities Subject to paragraph (2), a private entity shall be excluded from the definition of a debt collector, pursuant to the exception provided in section 1692a(6) of this title, with respect to the operation by the entity of a program described in paragraph (2)(A) under a contract described in paragraph (2)(B). (2) Conditions of applicability Paragraph (1) shall apply if— (A) a State or district attorney establishes, within the jurisdiction of such State or district attorney and with respect to alleged bad check violations that do not involve a check described in subsection (b), a pretrial diversion program for alleged bad check 15 USC 1692p 15 USC 1692o 15 USC 1692n 20 § 818 15 USC 1692p offenders who agree to participate voluntarily in such program to avoid criminal prosecution; (B) a private entity, that is subject to an administrative support services contract with a State or district attorney and operates under the direction, supervision, and control of such State or district attorney, operates the pretrial diversion program described in subparagraph (A); and (C) in the course of performing duties delegated to it by a State or district attorney under the contract, the private entity referred to in subparagraph (B)— (i) complies with the penal laws of the State; (ii) conforms with the terms of the contract and directives of the State or district attorney; (iii) does not exercise independent prosecutorial discretion; (iv) contacts any alleged offender referred to in subparagraph (A) for purposes of participating in a program referred to in such paragraph— (I) only as a result of any determination by the State or district attorney that probable cause of a bad check violation under State penal law exists, and that contact with the alleged offender for purposes of participation in the program is appropriate; and (II) the alleged offender has failed to pay the bad check after demand for payment, pursuant to State law, is made for payment of the check amount; (v) includes as part of an initial written communication with an alleged offender a clear and conspicuous statement that— (I) the alleged

offender may dispute the validity of any alleged bad check violation; (II) where the alleged offender knows, or has reasonable cause to believe, that the al- 21 § 818 15 USC 1692p leged bad check violation is the result of theft or forgery of the check, identity theft, or other fraud that is not the result of the conduct of the alleged offender, the alleged offender may file a crime report with the appropriate law enforcement agency; and (III)if the alleged offender notifies the private entity or the district attorney in writing, not later than 30 days after being contacted for the first time pursuant to clause (iv), that there is a dispute pursuant to this subsection, before further restitution efforts are pursued, the district attorney or an employee of the district attorney authorized to make such a determination makes a determination that there is probable cause to believe that a crime has been committed; and (vi) charges only fees in connection with services under the contract that have been authorized by the contract with the State or district attorney.
(b) Certain checks excluded A check is described in this subsection if the check involves, or is subsequently found to involve—

(1) a postdated check presented in connection with a payday loan, or other similar transaction, where the payee of the check knew that the issuer had insufficient funds at the time the check was made, drawn, or delivered; (2) a stop payment order where the issuer acted in good faith and with reasonable cause in stopping payment on the check; (3) a check dishonored because of an adjustment to the issuer's account by the financial institution holding such account without providing notice to the person at the time the check was made, drawn, or delivered; (4) a check for partial payment of a debt where the payee had previously accepted partial payment for such debt; 22 § 818 15 USC 1692p (5) a check issued by a person who was not competent, or was not of legal age, to enter into a legal contractual obligation at the time the check was made, drawn, or delivered; or (6) a check issued to pay an obligation arising from a transaction that was illegal in the jurisdiction of the State or district attorney at the time the check was made, drawn, or delivered. (c) Definitions For purposes of this section, the following definitions shall apply:

(1) State or district attorney The term "State or district attorney" means the chief elected or appointed prosecuting attorney in a district, county (as defined in section 2 of title 1), municipality, or comparable jurisdiction, including State attorneys general who act as chief elected or appointed prosecuting attorneys in a district, county (as so defined), municipality or comparable jurisdiction, who may be referred to by a variety of titles such as district attorneys, prosecuting attorneys, commonwealth's attorneys, solicitors, county attorneys, and state's attorneys, and who are responsible for the prosecution of State crimes and violations of jurisdiction-specific local ordinances. (2) Check The term "check" has the same meaning as in section 5002(6) of title 12. (3) Bad check violation The term "bad check violation" means a violation of the applicable State criminal law relating to the writing of dishonored checks. § 819. Effective date This title takes effect upon the expiration of six months after the date of its enactment, but section 809 shall apply only with respect to debts for which the initial attempt to collect occurs after such effective date. 15 USC 1692 note 23 Printed May 2013 Legislative History House Report: No. 95-131 (Comm. on Banking, Finance, and Urban Affairs) Senate Report: No. 95-382 (Comm. on Banking, Housing and Urban Affairs) Congressional Record, Vol. 123 (1977) April 4, House considered and passed H.R. 5294. Aug. 5, Senate considered and passed amended version of H.R. 5294. Sept. 8, House considered and passed Senate version. Enactment: Public Law 95-109 (September 20, 1977) Amendments: Public Law Nos. 99-361 (July 9, 1986) 101-73 (August 9, 1989) 102-242 (December 19, 1991) 102-550 (October 28, 1992) 104-88 (December 29, 1995) 104-208 (September 30, 1996) 109-351 (October 13, 2006) 111-203 (July 21, 2010)

There you have it, that is the whole Fair Credit reporting Act of 1970

Now you know why I broke down the main parts for you. You have all the information needed to fix or repair your credit.

Remember that fair credit reporting affects all of us and intentional misleading of your credit reporting is frowned on.

We all need to work together for a better tomorrow.

I am sure you realize you got a deal, why is this book so affordable? Well it's mainly because I am on your side, I want you to better your situation and get all that you deserve.

I hope you choose to hold on to this book and if you know anyone that needs a copy, that you tell them where to get their own copy.

This is a life tool, a reference guide you can use over and over. Put it somewhere safe and when you need it, you know where to find it.

I will leave you with some ideas on how to build good credit lines and how to maintain old ones.

Chapter 7
Putting it to use.

Well you're on your way to repairing your credit. I have some tips you can use to help add positive credit and maintain your credit for the long haul.

Most people don't know the information this book offers. Information that will give you an edge in life that others do not have.

So, you have a choice now, do you use this book and pass it on to someone else or should you hold on to it and keep it for future use?

Understanding a system that will help you buy a home, a car or something else in your life is a lifelong tool that will continue to help you get on track.

My recommendation is that you hold on to this book for future use but offer the information in it or tell your friend or family member where to buy their own copy.

This is a potential gift that could change someone's life and perhaps the best fourteen dollars you ever spent.

Why did I call the book "A Fair Guide to Credit Repair"? Fair is a funny word; everyone has their own set up rules they have constructed for themselves a set of rules they live by. What is fair to one person may not be fair to another. Fairness, is it fair that someone can buy a home and you can't because you made a few mistakes that keep creeping up and destroying your chances to have a happy life? Everyone deserves a home, a place they can live and build their life around.

Few reach this dream because they are not provided with the
tools to succeed in life.

Life is everchanging sometimes we have problems,
sometimes everything seems to fall into place, and
sometimes you need to make things happen and that is where
this book finds its value.

I learned a lot writing this book and gathering the
information to pass on to you the reader. Not everything in
this book will help you and there are no guarantees that
everything is going to instantly be better, but this is a start
and you are taking control of your life and that my friend is
priceless.

My Ideas to further help your credit

Notes from the Author

Rent to own stores are a terrible way to buy things because you will spend an enormous amount of money on purchases.

People that suffer with bad credit have little to no choice other than layaway to buy the things they need, and few people have the patience to buy goods and services that way.

If you are using Rent to Own to buy items and you are paying on time you can use the forms I included in the book / kit to add this as positive credit to your report.

Anything you ever purchased from rent to own stores "if your pay history is good", you should add as positive credit. Most rent to own companies do not report your payments to a credit bureau unless you don't pay them.

Why? It's simple they want to keep you buying from them. Why help you get good credit and give you better options. It's all about the money, your money!

If you do not pay them, they will punish you for 7 years by reporting it to your credit agencies forcing you to have no other choice but to use their services again and again.

Wow 7 years is a bit extreme for a late payment on washing machine as an example. This is a one-sided credit line and it is up to you to report it as a two-sided credit line.

You can also put notes into your credit file as to why you missed the payment.

There are companies like ©Fingerhut that will report to credit agencies and that is a great way to build credit.

The next time you need a pair of pants buy online and pay your payments on time or before. Allowing you to build small credit lines and push the bad credit to the back of the report.

Why is that important? You want potential creditors to see you have changed your habits and are now paying for the items you buy and more importantly you are paying on time.

Here's another idea!

You can often give your bank $500.00 buy a CD and then borrow against the CD using it as a secured loan. Sign up for a bank account, set up auto pay and forget about it until its paid for.

Every payment will be on time because it's on autopay. This is a very low-cost way to pay on a line of credit and once it is paid for you can cash in the CD or do it again and again.

Looking for ways to improve your situation sometimes takes out of the box thinking. Remember that sometimes the best things in life are found on the other side of fear.

.

Good credit is like raising a child it needs to be watched, nourished and well taken care of for it to grow. Once your credit score gets better, so does your quality of life.

Don't buy a car from buy here pay here lot's they are basically the same as rent to Own stores.

If you have no other choice and you pay on time report your payments to the credit bureau as positive credit, there is a form included in this book to do that.

There are likely loads of other ways to build credit but like I said before this is a guide to help you get started and if you use it properly it can change your life.

I truly hope you will apply what you have learned to get back on track and enjoy life a little more.

A lot of this book you may have already known but if you learned one new thing, it was worth every penny you spent on it.

Good Luck!

NOTES

NOTES

NOTES

www.ingramcontent.com/pod-product-compliance
Lightning Source LLC
Chambersburg PA
CBHW051412250726
48655CB00003B/1012